Bowing Variations for the Cello

Book One

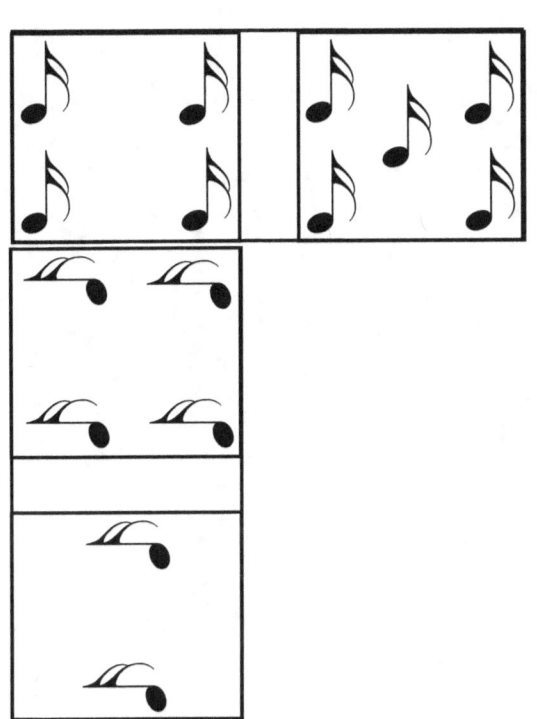

by Cassia Harvey

CHP136

©2005 by C. Harvey Publications All Rights Reserved.

www.charveypublications.com - print books
www.learnstrings.com - PDF downloadable books
www.harveystringarrangements.com - chamber music

Bowing Variations

BOOK ONE

Cassia Harvey

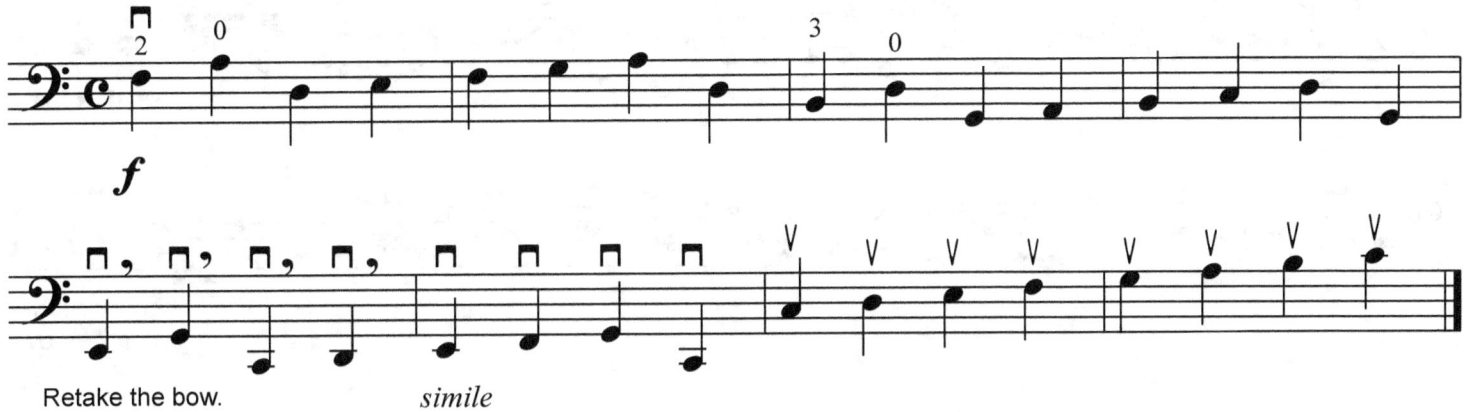

©2005 C. Harvey Publications All Rights Reserved.

9. **Use the fingers and wrist (more than the arm) to change bow direction here.**

10. **Use the fingers and wrist (more than the arm) to change bow direction here.**

Repeat at the tip of the bow.

11.

©2005 C. Harvey Publications All Rights Reserved.

17.

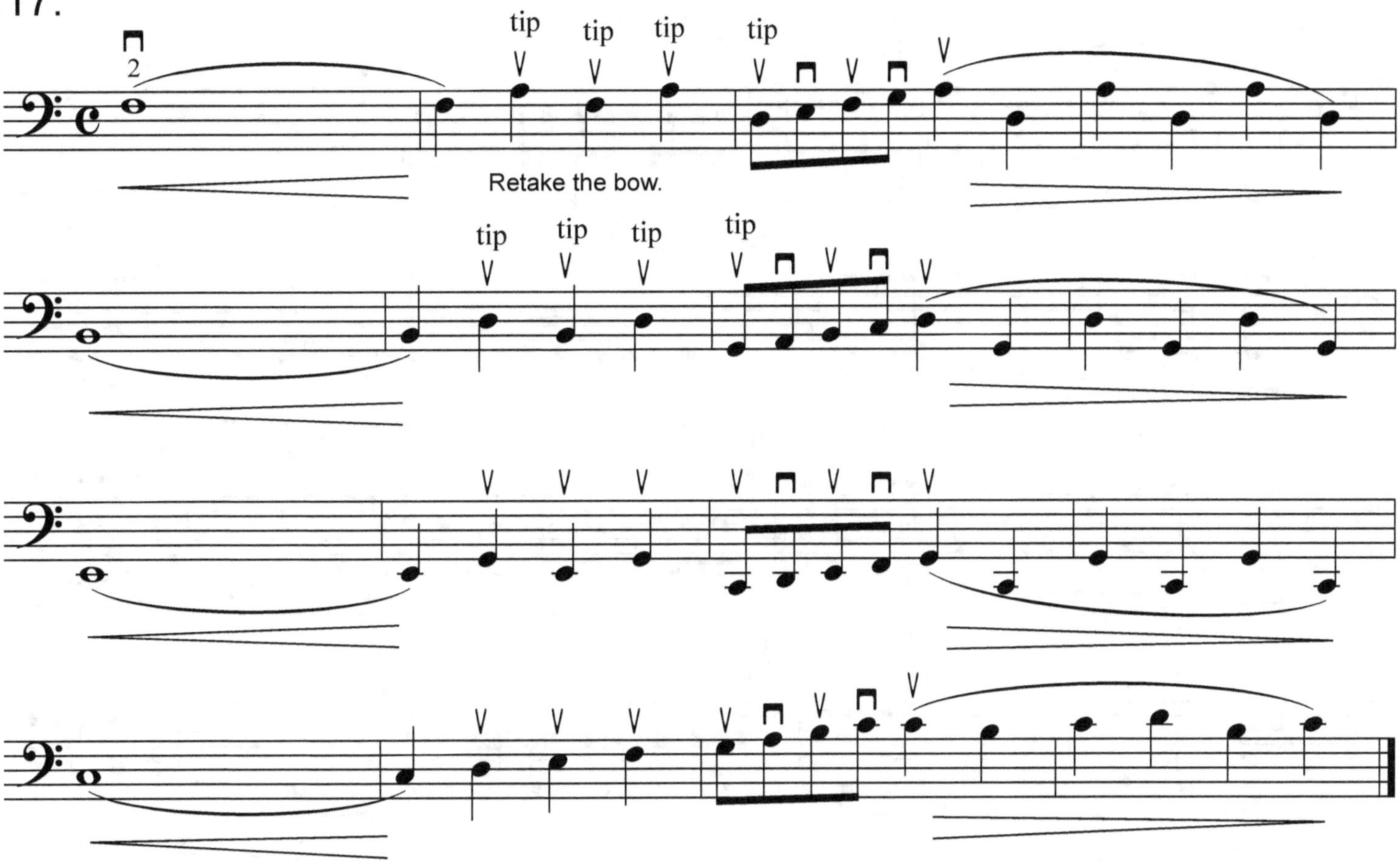

Retake the bow.

18. **Use the fingers and wrist (more than the arm) to change bow direction here.**

Presto

19.

20. **Use the fingers and wrist (more than the arm) to change bow direction here.**

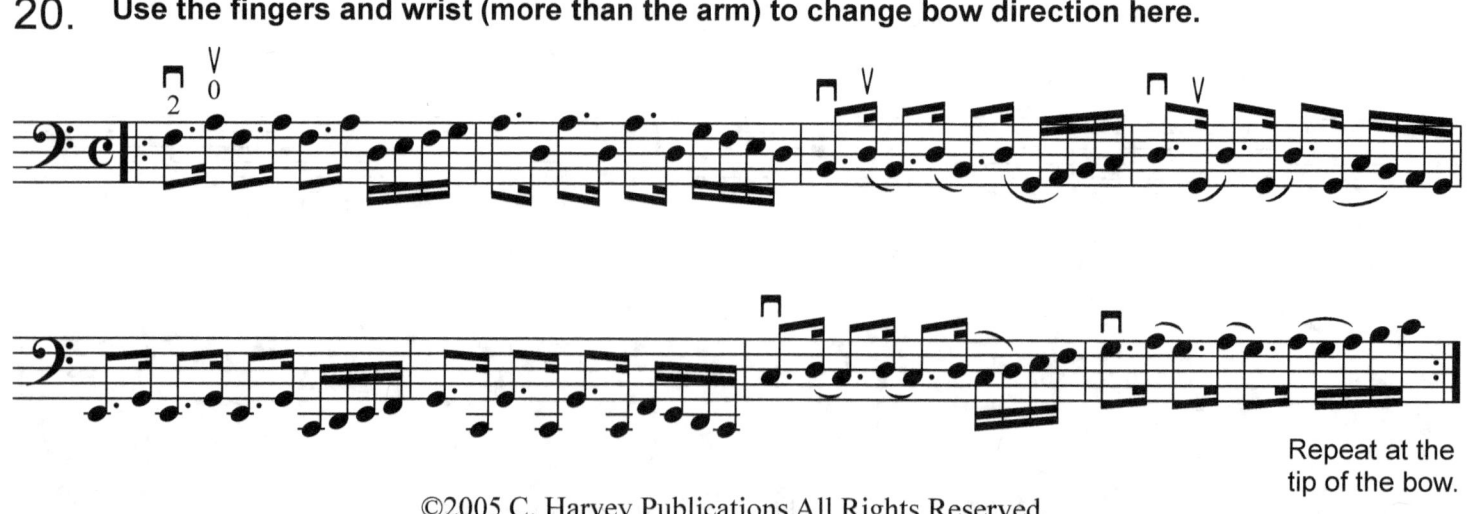

Repeat at the tip of the bow.

30.

31.

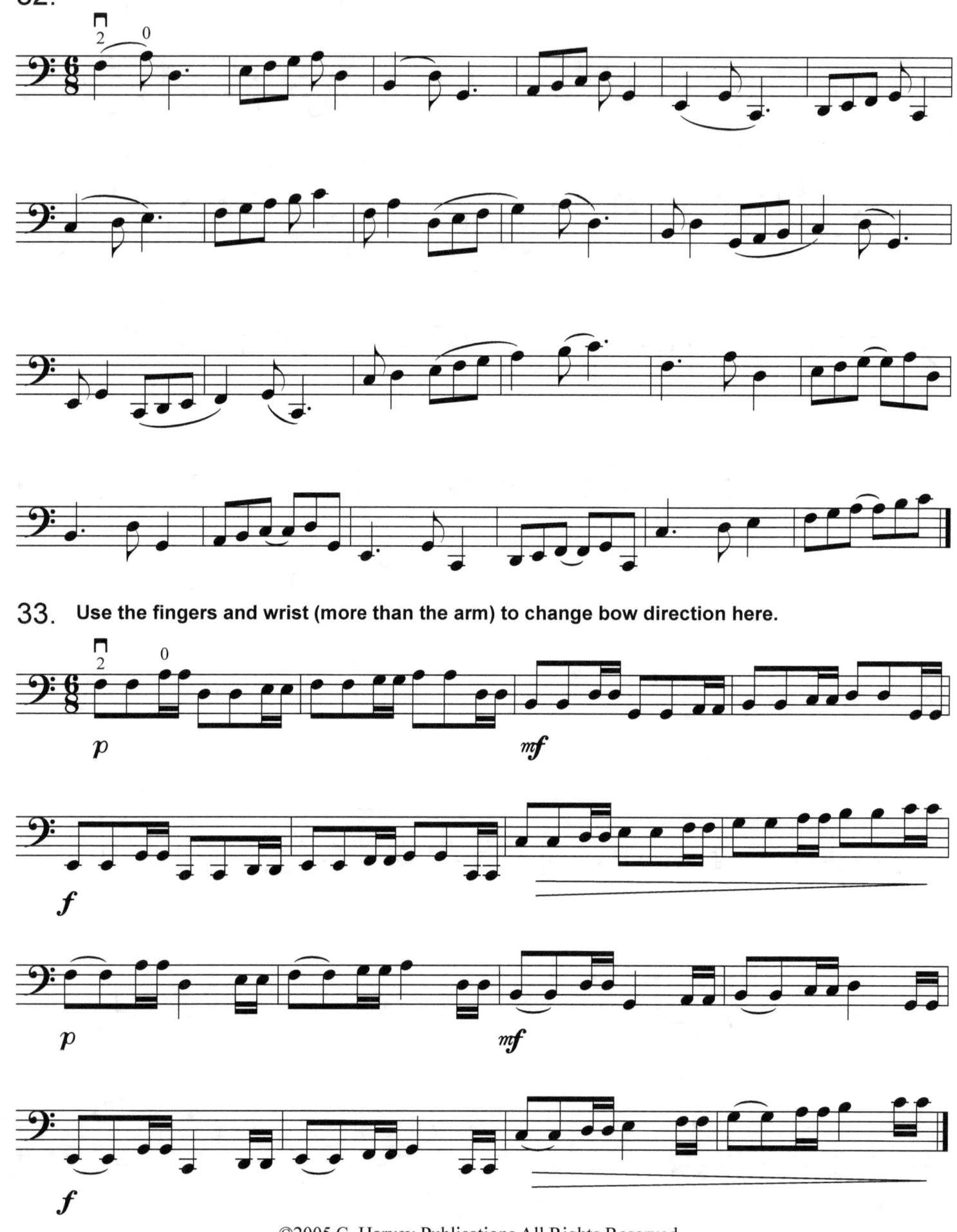

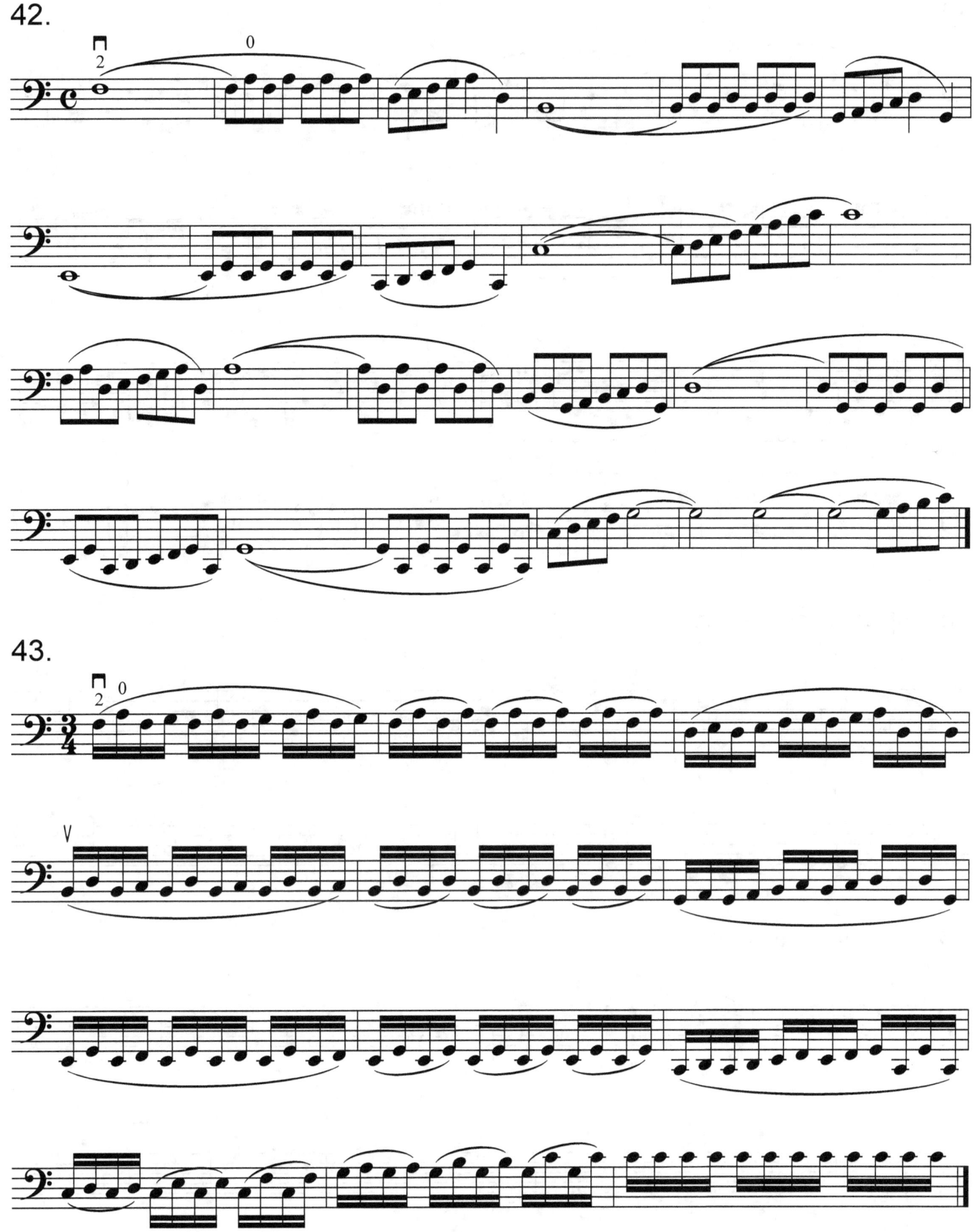

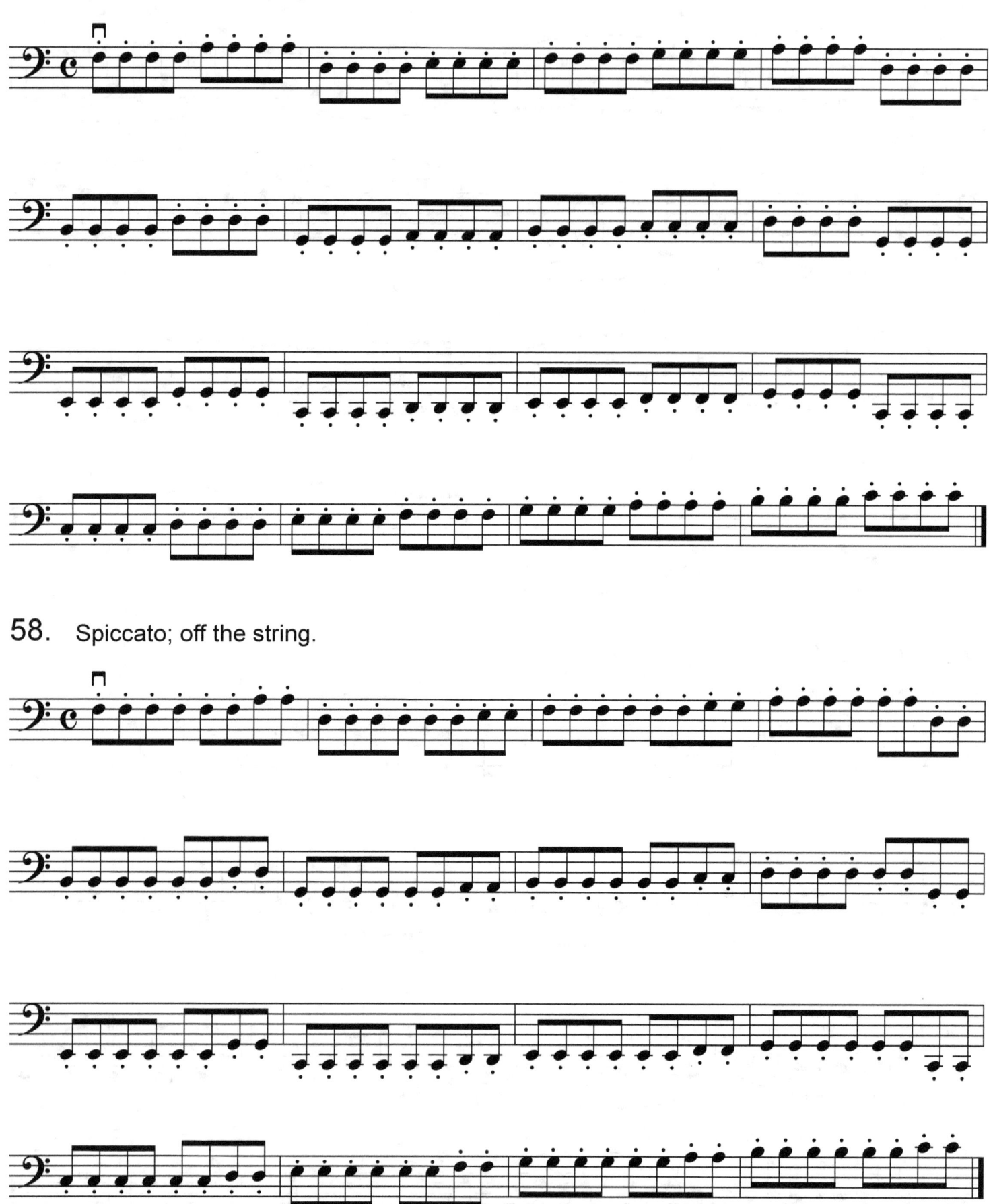

57. Spiccato; off the string.

58. Spiccato; off the string.

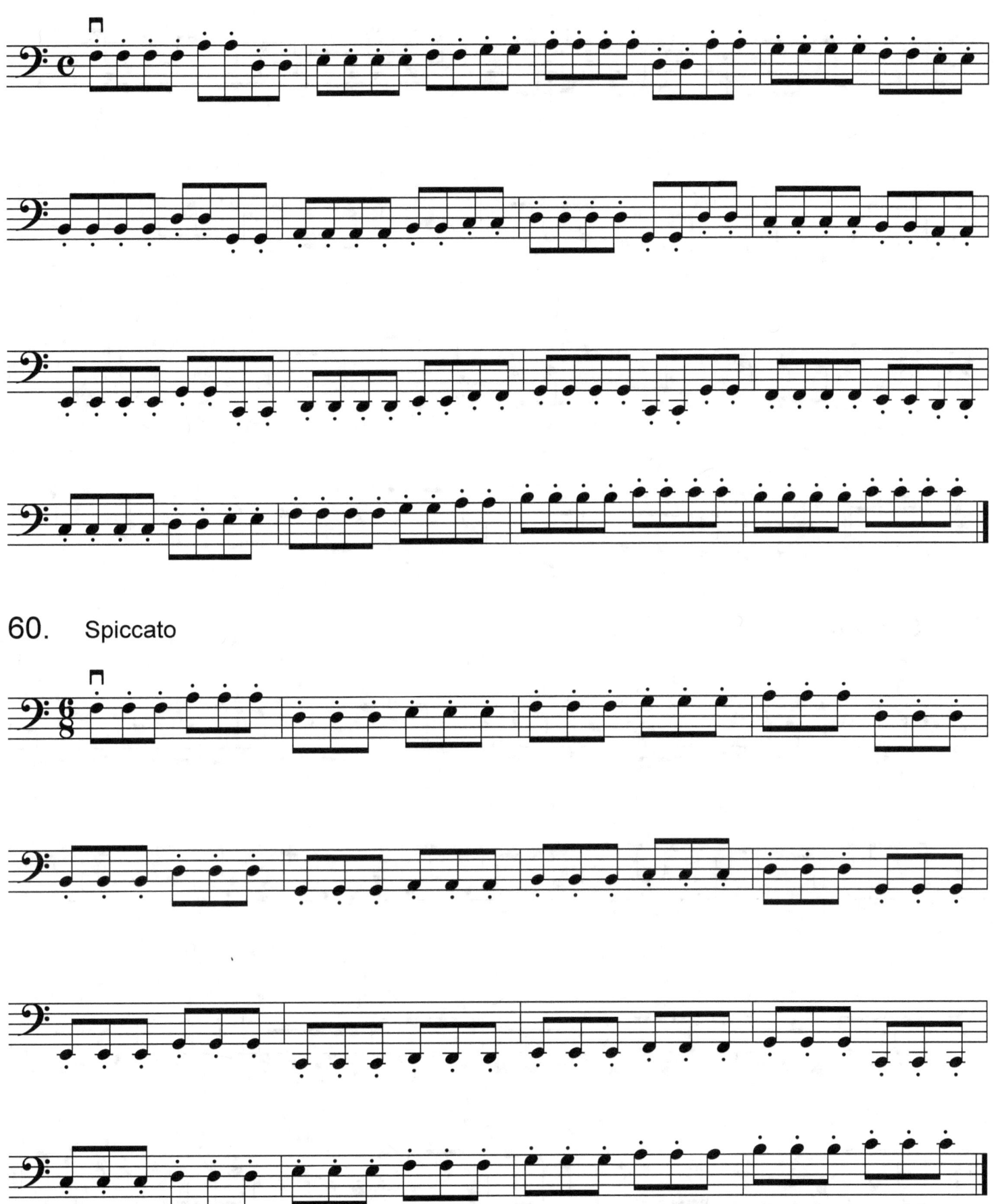

61. Spiccato

62. Spiccato

65. Spiccato; off the string

66. Spiccato; off the string

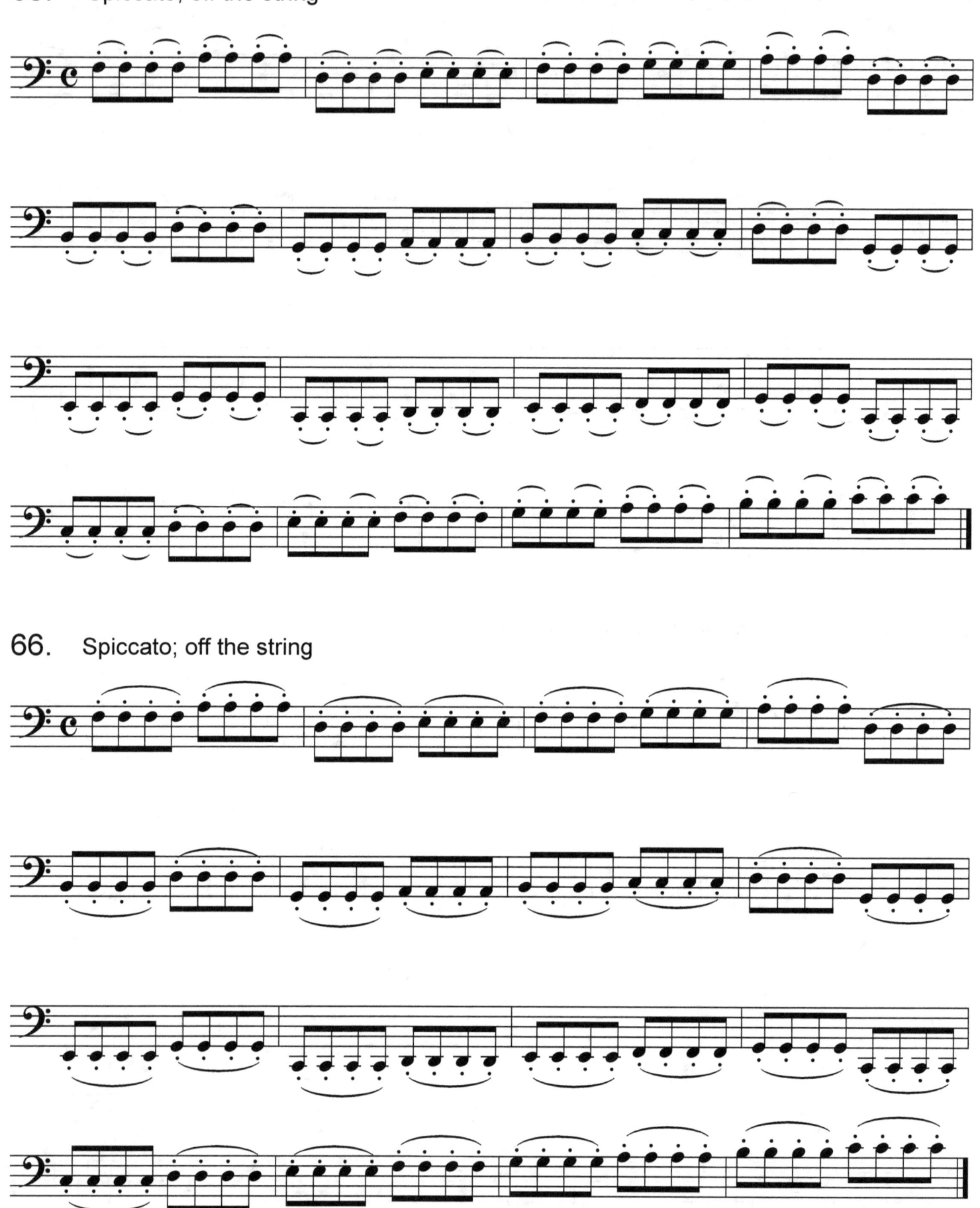

69. Dots here are Spiccato; off the string.

70. First smooth slurs, then Spiccato (off the string) on the dots.

©2005 C. Harvey Publications All Rights Reserved.

71. The up-bows are Spiccato (off the string.)

72. Use the fingers and wrist (more than the arm) to change bow direction here.

73.

74. Use the fingers and wrist (more than the arm) to change bow direction here.

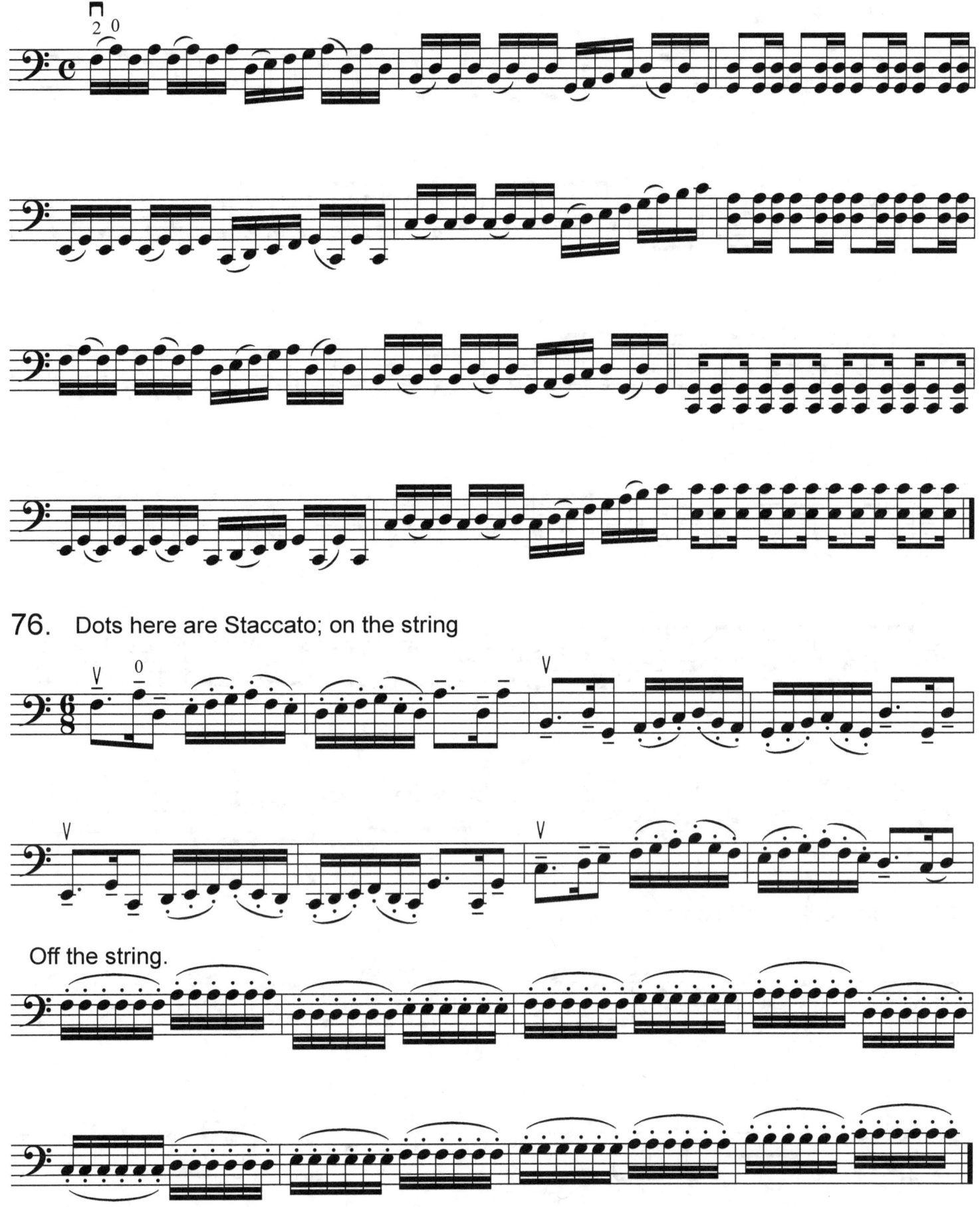

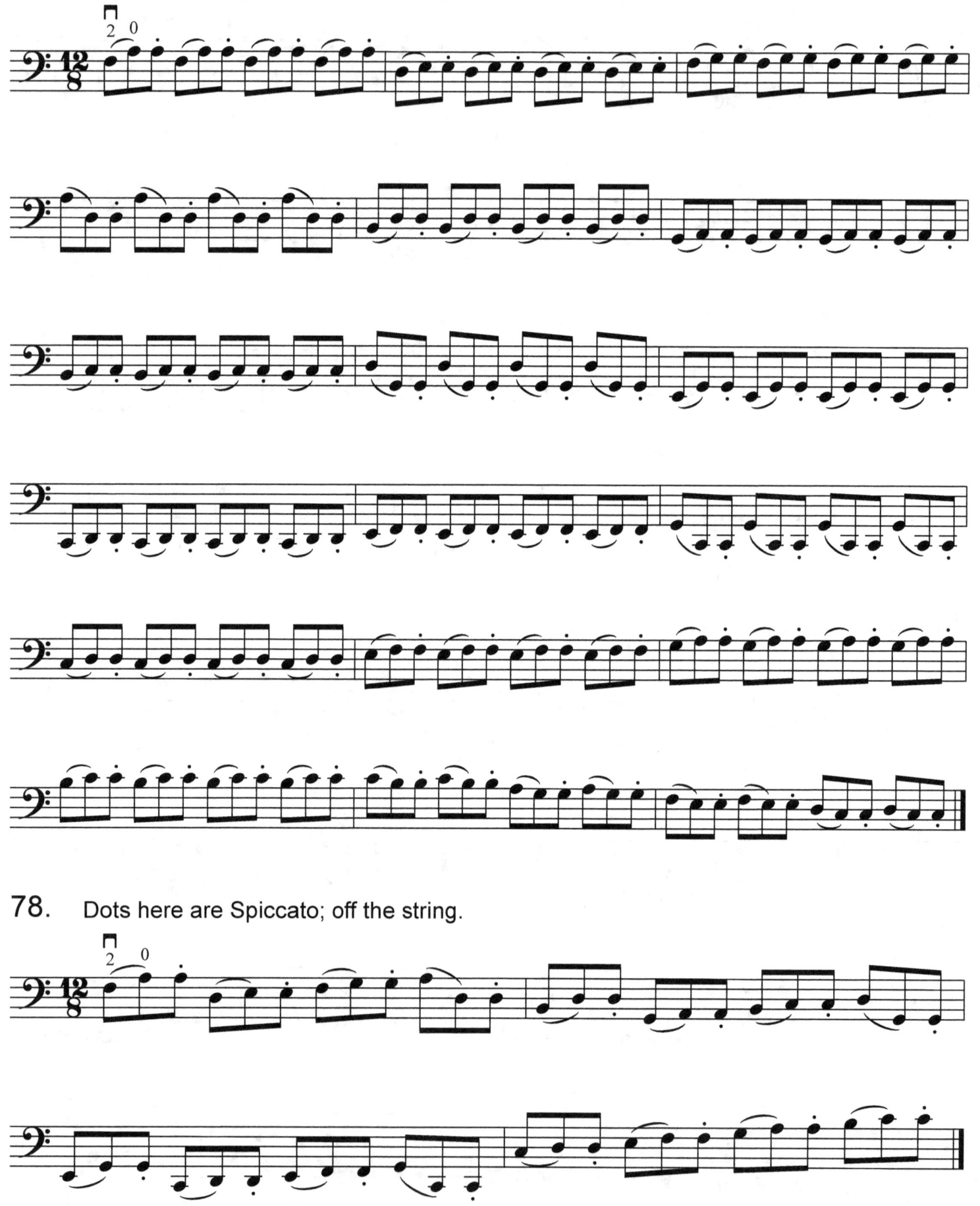

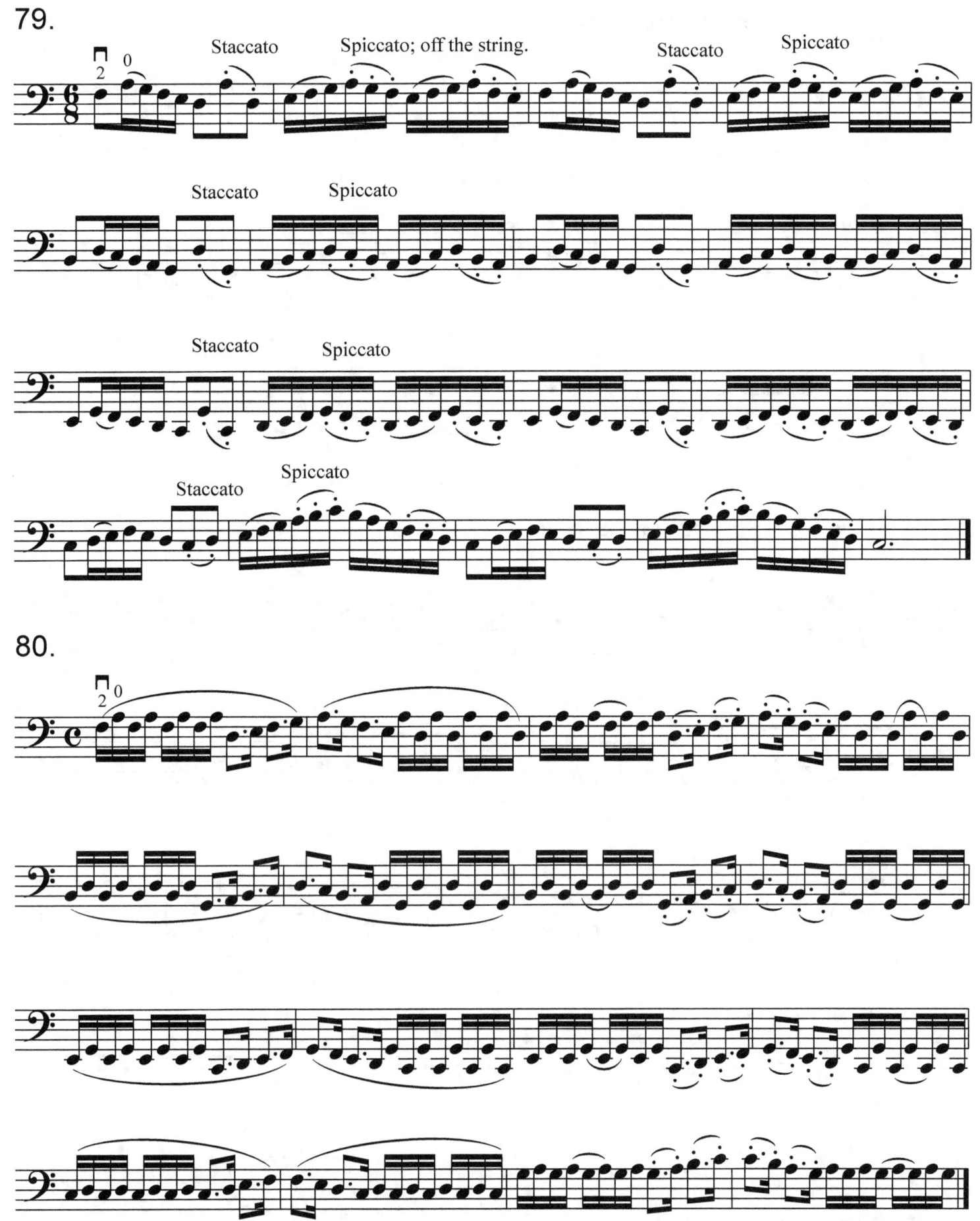

81. Dots here are Spiccato; off the string.

82. Dots here are Spiccato; off the string.

87. **Use the fingers and wrist (more than the arm) to change bow direction here.**

Retake the bow. *simile*

88. **Use the fingers and wrist (more than the arm) to change bow direction here.**

89. Use the fingers and wrist (more than the arm) to change bow direction here.

90. Use the fingers and wrist (more than the arm) to change bow direction here.

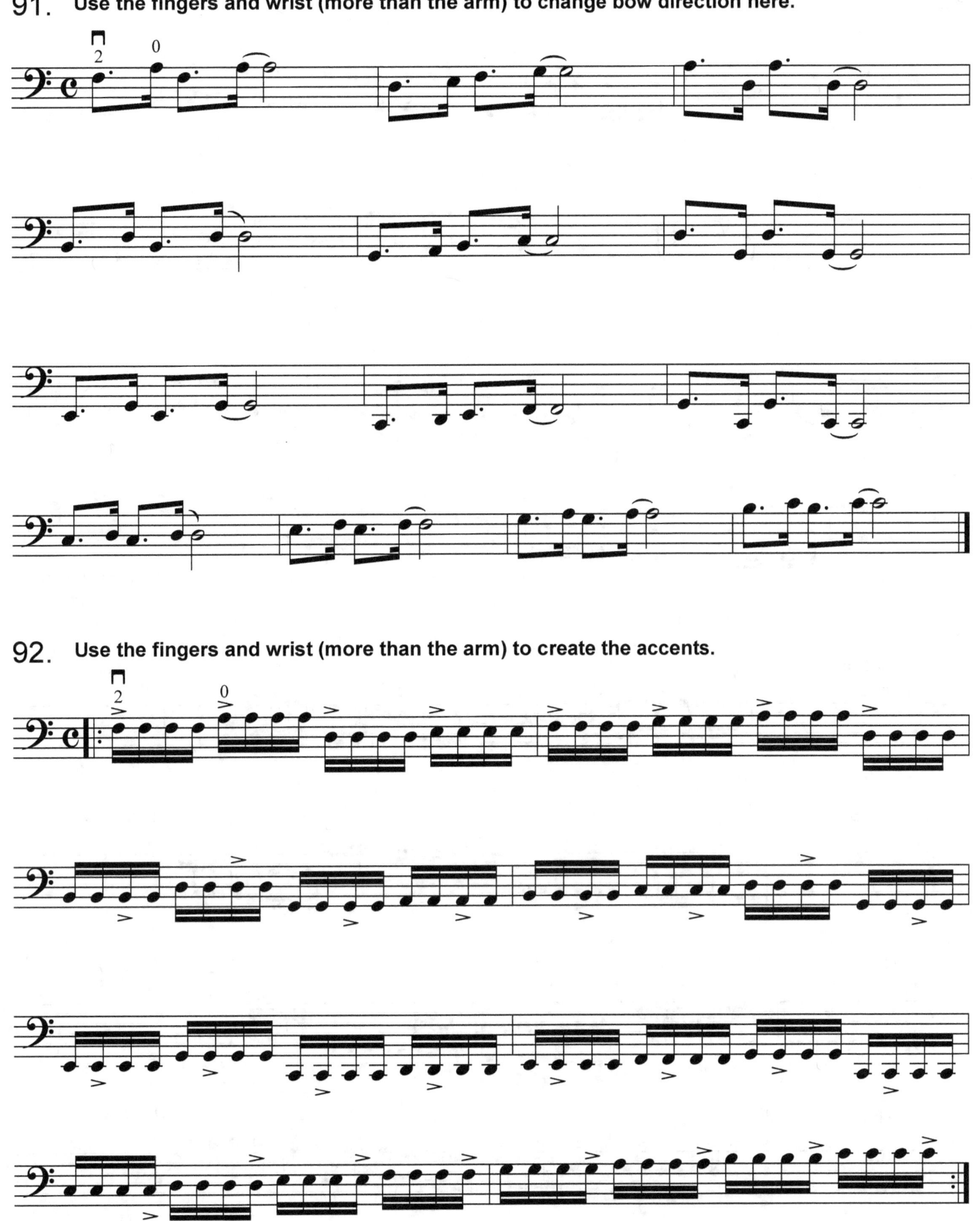

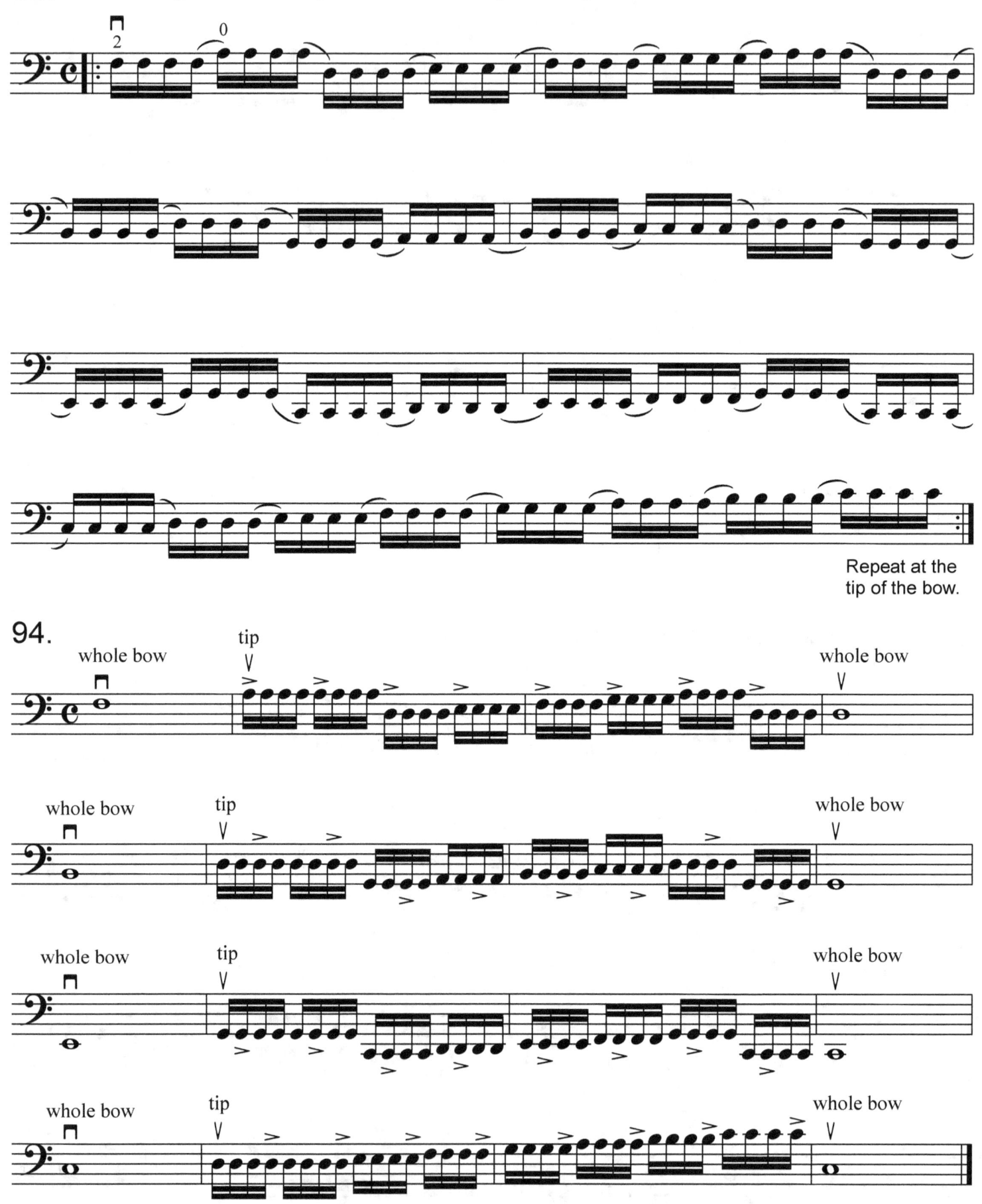

95. **Use the fingers and wrist (more than the arm) to change bow direction here.**

Repeat at the tip of the bow.

96. **Use the fingers and wrist (more than the arm) to change bow direction here.**

Repeat at the tip of the bow.

97. **Use the fingers and wrist (more than the arm) to change bow direction here.**

98. **Use the fingers and wrist (more than the arm) to change bow direction here.**

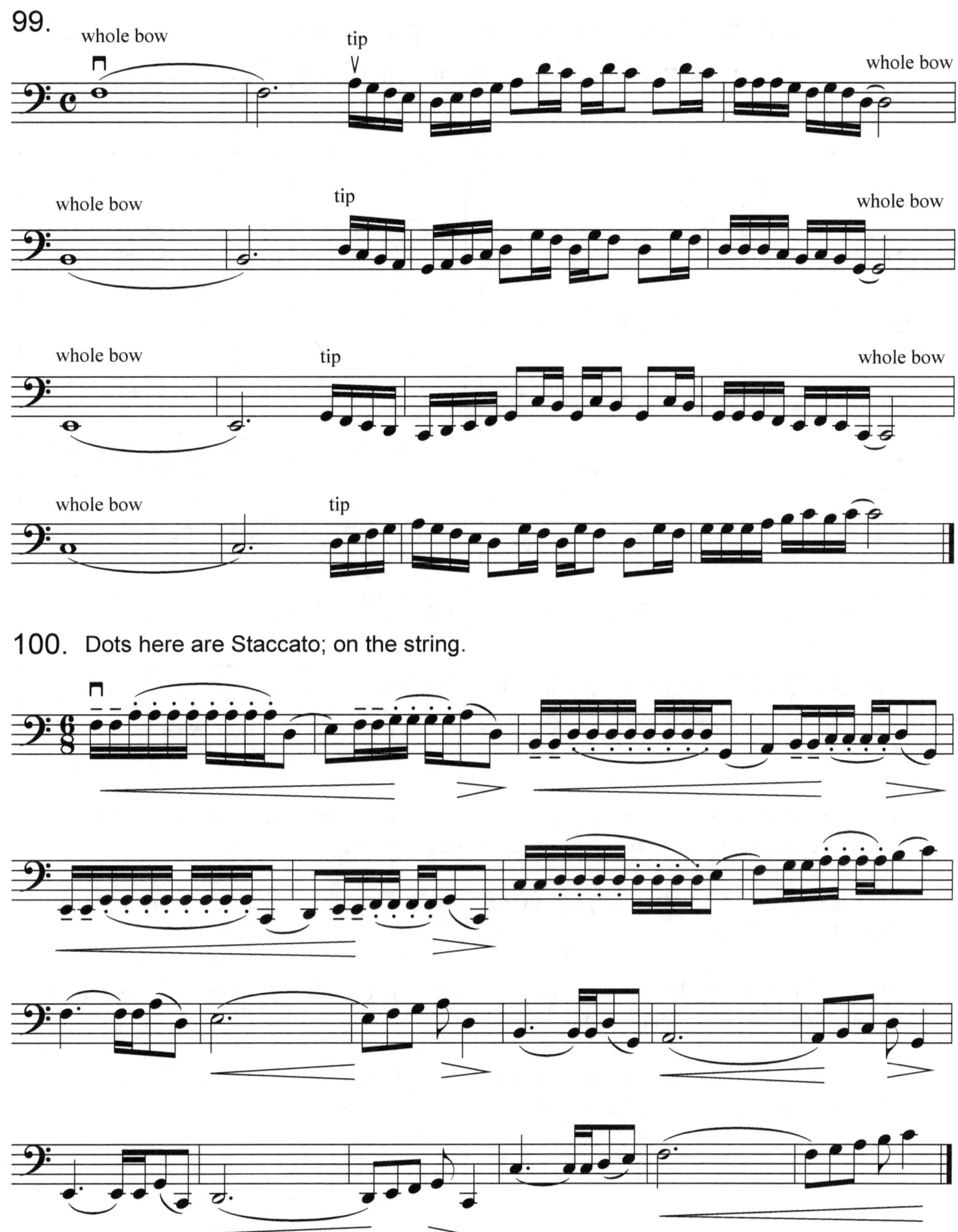

Also available from www.charveypublications.com: CHP351 Open String Bow Workouts for Cello, Book One

This book of new and exciting bowing workouts for the cello gives you 97 exercises to train your bow on open strings before you begin the rest of your practice.

Since there are no left hand notes, you can focus entirely on improving the dexterity and control of the right (bow) hand.

Useful also for students who are struggling with reading notes, this book gives cellists a tremendous resource for creating better tone.

The exercises work on on bow distribution, rests and retaking bows, slurs, triplets, dotted rhythms, double stops, string crossing and more.

www.ingramcontent.com/pod-product-compliance
Lightning Source LLC
Chambersburg PA
CBHW051425070526
44584CB00023B/3579